Healthy Relationships

By

Julie W. Hubbs, M.S.

ISBN: 979-8-3517-3707-2

Copyright 2022, Julie W. Hubbs

Hubbs, Julie W.

Healthy Relationships

Cover designer: Julie W. Hubbs

Dedicated to the Soaring Eagles who survive by living on higher ground:

Lee

Richard B.

Richard R.

Robin

Introduction

The benefits of a healthy relationship are a valuable contribution to today's society. We live in a world where the family unit is strained with the advent of technology, and this puts a strain on the roles within many of our personal and professional relationships.

Respect and trust are the building blocks of a healthy relationship, and the various ways we demonstrate to others that we love them plays a major role in how we form these relationships.

Also playing a role in building healthy relationships is the respect for the autonomy of others, while we ensure our own autonomy is respected as well.

This workbook is intended not to be an instructional book on relationships, but as a workbook and focus aid for open and real discussion about what a healthy relationship is between people, and how to foster and grow these relationships into mutual love and respect.

Take time to think about the questions being asked in this workbook and then answer the questions thoroughly and in detail. Use extra pieces of paper, if necessary. ***The more effort you put into your answers, the more positive benefits you will receive.***

- Coach

Table of Contents

Chapter 1: Personal Inventory	1
Chapter 2: Respect Is Earned	13
Chapter 3: Balance Is Harmony	17
Chapter 4: Boundaries Define How You Want To Be Treated	24
Chapter 5: Denial Is Real and Needs Attention	37
Chapter 6: Trusting Relationships	46
Chapter 7: Active Listening	50
Chapter 8: Signs of a Loving Relationship	54

Chapter 1: Personal Inventory

1) Give three to five reasons why you want to participate in this program?

   a) _____
   _____
   _____
   _____
   _____
   _____

b)

c)

d)

e) _____
   _____
   _____
   _____
   _____
   _____
   _____

2) At what age did you realize that males and females are different?

   _____
   _____
   _____
   _____
   _____

3) What age did you begin dating?

   _____
   _____
   _____
   _____
   _____

4) If you are or have been married, on a scale of zero to ten what is or was your marital satisfaction?

_____
_____
_____
_____
_____
_____
_____

5) Did either you or your spouse participate in extra marital affairs? Who? Did your partner catch you or did you catch them? Did you or your partner confess?

_____
_____
_____
_____
_____
_____
_____
_____
_____
_____
_____

6) If there was cheating, did the relationship survive? How?

_____
_____
_____
_____
_____
_____
_____
_____
_____

7) Describe your current social situation. Do you have a spouse? Girlfriend? Boyfriend? Both?

_____
_____
_____
_____
_____
_____
_____
_____
_____

8) Have you met anyone through the internet? If so, explain the situation.

9) What did you learn about relationships from your parents?

10) What did your parents teach you about love?

_____
_____
_____
_____
_____
_____
_____
_____

11) What did your parents teach you about marriage?

_____
_____
_____
_____
_____
_____
_____
_____

12) What did your parents teach you about being a man (or woman)?

_____
_____
_____
_____
_____
_____
_____

13) As a teenager how were you influenced by your friends regarding sex, relationships, and intimacy?

_____
_____
_____
_____
_____
_____
_____
_____

14) How have you been influenced by your intimate partners in the areas of sexual relations and your relationship style?

_____
_____
_____
_____
_____
_____
_____
_____

15) How did your mother interact with you? Was it a healthy relationship?

_____
_____
_____
_____
_____
_____
_____
_____

16) How did your father interact with you? Was it a healthy relationship?

_____
_____
_____
_____
_____
_____
_____

17) How did your family (grandparents, aunts, uncles, siblings, or cousins) interact with you? Were they healthy relationships?

_____
_____
_____
_____
_____
_____
_____

18) What other factors influenced why you are the way you are in relationships and the way you have sex (e.g., church, media, peer pressure, pornography, etc.)?

_____
_____
_____
_____
_____
_____
_____
_____

19) Do you interact with others in a way that is like the way your mother, your father, or your family interacted with you?

_____
_____
_____
_____
_____
_____
_____
_____

20) What is something you wish everyone knew about you?

_____
_____
_____
_____
_____
_____
_____
_____

We cannot force someone to hear a message they are not ready to receive. But we must never underestimate the power of planting a seed.

Chapter 2: Respect is Earned

- Recognize your partner is a whole person.
- Respect their space and their stuff.
- Speaking to one another in a way that is not offensive.
- Know that your partner has different experiences and opinions from you.
- Demonstrate mutual trust.
- Appreciate your differences.
- Get to know yourself first.
- Do not be dismissive of your partner.
- Be aware of when you are talking down to your partner or belittling.
- Do not embarrass your partner in public.
- Be kind and generous.
- Respect your partner's privacy.
- Do no harm.

"Be careful with your words. Once they are said, they can only be forgiven, not forgotten."

Respect means different things to different people. Some people believe it is admiration of another person. Other's respect people in authority such as parents, relatives, teachers, and even bosses. Then other times respect means upholding the thought that all people have the right to make up their own mind and make up their own decisions in order to feel safe in their daily lives.

Respect in a healthy relationship means partners are equals. This means neither partner has control or authority over the other person. Each person is free to live their own life and make their own decisions. They get to choose to share or not share aspects of their life. Respect also means you might not agree with your partner but it is your choice to trust them and have faith in their judgment or not. Most of the time this level of trust is built up over time as your relationship progresses. It is important to really take the time to get to know one another.

Some of the ways couples can show respect to one another in a healthy relationship are to:
- Talk openly and honestly to each other.
- Listen without thinking about what you want to say.

- Value each other's needs and feelings.
- Compromise, you don't always need to be right.
- Speak kindly to and about each other.
- Give each other space and privacy.
- Support each other's hobbies, interests, and careers, etc.
- Build each other up.
- Honor each other's boundaries, no matter what.

Respecting your partner is important, but so is having respect for yourself. Self-respect is the key to building confidence and keeping your relationship healthy. So, what is self-respect? It is when you can respect yourself, be genuine, and be an authentic person. This does not mean you think you are perfect; it means respect is deserved even though you are not perfect.

Everyone has worth and value. Self-respect means you hold yourself to your own set of standards and not worry about what others think about you or say behind your back. Self-respect means you are in control of your body and your mind.

Reading and learning, going to therapy, taking classes, eating healthy foods, moving in ways that makes your body feel better are some ways to honor who you are as a healthy person.

People will come and go in life, but the person in the mirror will be there forever: So **be good to yourself.**

Chapter 3: Balance is Harmony

People who are emotionally balanced are in control of their emotions and their behavior. They can handle life's challenges, build strong relationships, and recover from setbacks. But maintaining mental and emotional health takes effort.

Emotional balance is also referred to as emotional self-control. People with strengths in emotional balance find ways to manage their impulses and emotions, even in very stressful situations. Head-Heart-Gut alignment is a must.

A good sign of emotional stability is when someone often keeps their commitments. Their words and behaviors match most of the time.

Relationships go through ebbs and flows, sometimes daily, and riding them through is how balance is maintained. A balanced relationship is a healthy relationship. It is about being equal partners and making sure each person is feeling comfortable and supported. It is also important each person has a sense of independence.

Three red flags in any relationship are physical, emotional, or mental abuse. Red flags are warning signs that indicate unhealthy or manipulative behavior. When you encounter red flags, it is best to pause and reflect on what is really going on in the relationship. Cultivating self-awareness of red flags can help keep you from getting hurt emotionally, mentally, or physically.

Red flags are often so subtle that people begin accepting them as common rather than warning signs. They then become open to emotional, psychological, and sometimes physical harm without realizing they are being abused.

Some red flags in any relationship are:

- Overly controlling behavior is a common red flag.

- Lack of trust in a relationship is a common red flag.

- Feelings of low self-esteem is a common red flag. The people closest to you need to be building you up not knocking you down.

- Emotional, or mental abuse is a common red flag that sometimes gets downplayed.

- Physical abuse is a red flag that should never be ignored.

- Substance abuse is a common red flag.

- Narcissism is a common red flag. Narcissistic personality disorder is a mental condition that indicates self-obsession, a misplaced sense of importance. Narcissists believe that the world revolves around them. If anyone threatens this belief, turmoil, and chaos tend to follow. Being involved with an ego driven person is exhausting and often traumatizing to others. Their needs will always be considered more important than yours.

- Anger management issues are a common red flag.

- Codependency is a common red flag issue.

- Inability to resolve conflicts is a common red flag issue.

- Constant jealousy is a common red flag issue.

- Gaslighting is a common tactic of manipulation. It is an insidious form of emotional abuse in which the manipulator will make you question your own sanity or judgements. Gaslighting is a huge red flag in any relationship.

- Lack of emotional intelligence is the ability to perceive and manage emotions. People with a low level of emotional intelligence cannot pick up on other people's feelings and therefore cannot easily empathize with you.

- Negatively affecting your other important relations such as family and friends is a common red flag. Healthy relationships should never come at the cost of your other important relationships.

Yellow flags are like the above-mentioned red flags but less severe. Yellow flags are an indication that there are problem areas that need to be addressed. Yellow flags indicate some areas that need to be shifted for the relationship to be healthy and flourish.

A red flag warning might be a partner who forbids you from going to a party at your sister's house without them. A yellow flag warning could be your partner becoming grumpy, moody, or angry when you do.

Yellow flags do not mean the relationship can't be healthy, it merely means there are areas to work on. But both partners must acknowledge work needs to be done and both people need to provide input to resolve the issues.

What are some yellow flag issues you have noticed either in your current relationships or in past relationships?

_____
_____
_____
_____
_____
_____
_____
_____
_____
_____
_____
_____
_____
_____
_____
_____

Best ways to tackle red and yellow flags are:

- Use tact.
- Know your own value and do not compromise it.
- Be honest with yourself and others.
- Practice self-care.
- Acknowledge your own needs.
- Communicate.
- Avoid being overly emotional.
- Avoid minimizing negative behaviors.
- Seek professional help.
- Set and stick to your boundaries.
- Reconnect with family and friends.
- Know when to call it quits and leave.

Healthy relationship goals:

- Coexisting with another person in a healthy manner.
- Getting your needs met.
- Discussing your needs.
- Listening to your partner's needs.
- Bargaining.
- Equal partners.
- Both feeling supported.
- Both feeling comfortable.
- Accept you will have disagreements.
- Build trust.
- Do not be too dependent on your partner.
- Do no harm.

Decide what kind of life you want. Then say no to everything that isn't that.

Chapter 4: Boundaries define how you want to be treated

Most of the time setting boundaries will greatly improve your life when you do it correctly. But, be aware, boundaries can also challenge people who love their power and control.

What is a boundary? A boundary is a limit. We set limits to protect the tender parts of ourselves. To set healthy boundaries you must be clear about what to include and what to leave out of your daily lives. The main purpose of setting boundaries is to take care of yourself and in so doing take care of your relationships.

Some boundaries to think about are:

- **Physical boundary**: Pay attention to what people are saying and what they are not saying. Hugging with some people is welcomed and with some people it is unwelcomed. Listen to what the person is telling you both verbally and nonverbally. Most people will be clear with their messages regarding if they want to be touched or not. If you are confused, it is okay to ask the person if they want to be touched.

Physical boundaries also include personal possessions such as phones, tablets, computers, homes, vehicles, clothing, office equipment, books, etc. The owner gets to decide what their boundary is around their possessions. If you are not the owner of these possessions you have no say, period.

- **Personal boundary**: A barrier of something you will or will not accept. For example, I will never be okay with someone being verbally or psychologically abusive to me.

- **Sexual boundary**: Men are more vulnerable before intercourse. Women are more vulnerable after intercourse. Men feel closest to their partner when they are having sex. Women feel closest to their partner before sex in order to feel sexual and sensual. If a couple has an argument, a man wants to have sex to reestablish their closeness and intimacy and the woman says,

"Are you crazy? We just had a huge fight. I am not in the mood for sex with you."

How do males and females who are in a relationship get on the same page romantically? To begin with, it's strongly recommended that two people give a future relationship time to build and grow before having sex. Get to really know one another first by building emotional trust.

Understand, there must be freedom in the relationship to say no. If a sexual experience is causing pain emotionally or physically, and someone wants to stop, understand no means no. Yes, it can be frustrating to stop, but respect the other person and stop.

Sexual safety is a must if you want a healthy relationship with your partner. To continue past a no, destroys all the trust you have built up.

- **Intimate boundary**: Close familiarity or friendship, closeness. Intimacy is closeness between people in personal relationships. It's what builds over time as you connect with someone, grow to care about each other, and feel more and more comfortable during your time together. It can include physical or emotional closeness, or even a mix of the two.

- **Financial boundary**: Many times, a couple has different views about money. Differences can include, how to save money, how to spend money, or how to earn money. It can also include, who pays the bills, who oversees investments, and who oversees household budgeting. Talking about money is extremely important, yet many couples never take the time to go over their wants and needs.

- **Emotional boundary**: Everyone deserves to be treated with respect and dignity. We honor ourselves by not allowing others to mistreat us. How does one navigate through emotional boundaries when everyone has different emotional boundaries? Usually, boundaries are created because of a person's past emotional issues. Past traumas can cause a person to feel insecure and a bit uncertain about opening their hearts up to others. Be sensitive and ask the other person how they are feeling and then really hear what they are saying. Also, take notice of their cues, for example, when you crack a certain type of joke do they shut down?

On the flip side make sure to remember you too have emotional boundaries that need to be considered. Maybe you grew up in an abusive household and may be very uncomfortable with put-downs, yelling, or destruction of property. Couples need to talk and share as much as possible in order to build trust in the relationship.

- **Time boundary**: Today you decided to spend the entire day cleaning the house. You did not plan anything else. First thing in the morning you drink some coffee, turned on some good music, pull out all the cleaning products, and start your day. Just as you are hitting your groove the doorbell rings. You look out the window and see it is your very verbal friend. You know from experience your friend will want to stay and visit for hours.

What would you do?

a) Drop everything and talk for hours?

b) Cut your friend off right in the beginning?

c) Compromise by giving her a cup of coffee, a one-hour chat, then hustle her out the door?

d) Ask your friend to help with the cleaning and then you can clean and visit at the same time?

There is no correct or incorrect answer. You must decide what your greatest need is.

- **Expectations**: Talk openly about what you want out of the relationship.

- **Intellectual**: Maybe one person in the relationship enjoys obtaining more training and education or requires stimulating intellectual conversations occasionally.

- **Devices** (phones, computers, texts, etc.): Maybe there needs to be some rules surrounding how long a person is using their devices. Will it be okay to look at one another's phones, computers, text messages, etc., or are they private?

- **Communication**: Sometimes emotions run high and one person or the other needs to take a time out or a break from the other person. This does not mean you get to leave the house and not come back for hours, it means perhaps you quietly read a book, or go for a walk, or work in the garden until things calm down. Then it is imperative that you and your partner come back together and communicate with one another. Talking through the problem is a must.

- **Compromise**: You are not always going to be the winner and you are not always going to be the loser. A healthy relationship is full of compromises sometimes several times a day. For example, who does what chores, where you will go to eat, who will do the grocery shopping, who watches the children most of the time, who cooks, etc.

- **Commitment:** Discuss the level of your commitment in the relationship. In what direction is your relationship headed and are you both on the same page?

- **Do no harm:** Don't harm yourself or the other person and do not allow yourself to be harmed.

Questions to consider when setting boundaries:

1) Am I putting another person's needs before mine?

_____
_____
_____
_____
_____
_____
_____
_____
_____
_____
_____
_____

2) Am I comfortable sharing a bank account with this person?

_____
_____
_____
_____
_____
_____
_____
_____
_____
_____

3) Am I risking my physical health being with this person?

4) Am I doing things that are emotionally or spiritually wrong for me?

5) Am I doing things that are intimately wrong for me?

_____
_____
_____
_____
_____
_____
_____

6) Am I doing things that are financially wrong for me?

_____
_____
_____
_____
_____
_____
_____

7) Am I doing things that are physically wrong for me?

_____
_____
_____
_____
_____
_____
_____

8) What physical boundaries make me feel safe?

_____
_____
_____
_____
_____
_____
_____
_____
_____
_____

9) What emotional boundaries make me feel safe?

_____
_____
_____
_____
_____
_____
_____
_____
_____
_____

10) How are some ways you have violated another person's boundaries?

_____
_____
_____
_____
_____
_____
_____

11) How are some ways you respected another person's boundaries?

_____
_____
_____
_____
_____
_____

12) Are there things you could have done better with regards to another person's boundaries?

_____
_____
_____
_____
_____
_____

13) Are there things you could have done better with regards to your own boundaries?

_____
_____
_____
_____
_____
_____

"Actions prove who someone is, words just prove who they pretend to be."

"The most precious gift you can give someone is the gift of your time and attention."

Chapter 5: Denial is real and needs attention

Some questions to start thinking about:

- Do you fight a lot?
- Are you happy?
- Are you still friends?
- Is your sex life nonexistent?
- Do you flirt with other people on a regular basis?
- Is there a lack of intimacy?
- Do you rationalize your problems away?
- Do you blame your partner?
- Do you compare your circumstances to others?
- Is the grass greener somewhere else?
- Do you feel hopeless about your future?
- Are you suspicious about your partner?
- Are you pulling away?
- How patient are you with your partner?

- Can you feel vulnerable?
- Are you willing to change yourself?
- Can you focus on the best parts of your relationship?

Denial is a defense mechanism that is used when you are faced with an extremely difficult situation. Without the proper skills it becomes easier to reject the truth even when there is overwhelming proof and evidence. In order to clearly understand your denial, you must look at what kind of a person you really are.

Are you a person with integrity? A person with integrity is honest, has strong moral principles, is aligned with their head, heart, and gut, and therefore can't be divided. You must be in balance and aligned with what is really the truth of a situation, not what you want or feel you need the truth to be.

Are you an honest person? Honesty is a must if you want to have integrity. Dishonesty and lying causes pain and suffering in yourself and in others.

Dishonesty ruins almost any opportunity to build trust in relationships.

Do you rationalize or justify your actions? People who say, "It wasn't my fault" or "They asked for it" are rationalizing and justifying their actions. Making excuses for inappropriate behaviors is wrong.

Do you minimize situations? It is wrong to minimize because it is often done when one person wants to manipulate and control another. Reasons for this behavior can range from an inability to empathize to not knowing how to validate others and express it effectively.

Minimizing basically is telling a person their experiences are not important. It is a form of abuse. Because it can be done in such a subtle manner, many people don't realize they are being abusive or are being abused. Then this style of communication becomes the norm. It is not good because emotional invalidation is the act of rejecting, dismissing, and minimizing a person's thoughts and feelings. It implies that person is not important.

When a person becomes aware that they are emotionally invalidating others they must understand their goal is to manipulate and control another individual. This behavior upsets the balance in what could be a healthy relationship.

It is Not My Job:

To fix other people.

To make sure you are liked.

To please everyone.

To do it all.

My Job is:

Self-love.

Love others.

Be authentic.

Speak my truth.

Be the best version of myself.

Breathe.

Exhale.

Here are some non-validating emotional statements:
- It wasn't that bad.
- It could be worse.
- Why are you crying?

- You shouldn't feel that way.
- Just get over it.
- Let it go.
- You are so sensitive.
- You are a drama queen.
- It's always about you.
- You have nothing to be mad about.

Invalidating effects causes emotional damage. It creates emotional distance, conflict, violence, and disruption in relationships. The recipient can feel alienated, confused, inferior, worthless, and hateful.

Ask yourself the hard questions, such as, are you an angry person? Anger is a choice and many angry people believe they're not out of control. Angry people would rather try to control others than work on themselves. It's easier to blame others for their angry outbursts, that way their anger can be justified and minimized.

Denial sets in and the behaviors become acceptable because "it's not my fault, they made me act this way." Angry people know exactly what they are doing and why. Their anger is a cover for some personal failure in their life that needs to be dealt with.

Understand that people will get angry, but you must learn to express anger in a healthy way. Properly understanding anger and then putting a calm voice to it builds trust in relationships.

a) How do you use denial in your life?

_____
_____
_____
_____
_____
_____
_____
_____
_____
_____

b) How has denial worked for you?

_____
_____
_____
_____
_____
_____
_____
_____
_____
_____

c) How has denial not worked for you?

_____
_____
_____
_____
_____
_____
_____
_____
_____
_____

d) Have you ever accepted responsibility in a relationship when you realized you were minimizing, justifying, or using denial?

_____
_____
_____
_____
_____
_____
_____
_____
_____
_____
_____

e) Describe the relationship you are currently involved in or would like to be involved in? Be very honest and use extra paper if needed.

_____
_____
_____
_____
_____
_____
_____
_____
_____
_____
_____
_____
_____

Nine Rules for True Apologies (unknown source)

A true apology:

1. Does not include the word but.
2. Keeps the focus on the apologizer's actions.
3. Does not overdo it with one's own pain and remorse.
4. Doesn't get caught up in who started what.
5. Is backed up by action to correct the situation.
6. Requires doing your best to avoid a repeat.
7. Is not used to avoid a difficult talk.
8. Does not risk making the hurt party feel worse in order to make the apologizer feel better.
9. Recognizes when "I'm sorry" is not enough and work is required to restore trust.

Chapter 6: Trusting Relationships

Emotional trust is the bedrock of a healthy relationship. It is self-knowledge. Knowing what is okay with you and what isn't; knowing where your blind spots are; knowing how to compensate for those blind spots; knowing you'll be okay if you walk away from someone you don't trust, or even if you stay and something goes wrong.

Trust is important in relationships because it allows you to be more open and giving. If you trust your partner and your partner trusts you, you are more likely to be forgiving of shortcomings or behaviors that irritate you, because overall you believe in one another and know you have each other's back.

- Why do we need trust? Trusting someone to do the right thing means you believe in their integrity and strength, to the extent that you are able to put yourself on the line, at some risk to yourself.

- Trust is essential to have an effective team, because it provides a great sense of safety.

- Can a relationship work without trust? Trust is one of the cornerstones of any healthy relationship, without it, two people cannot be comfortable with one another and the relationship will lack stability and safety.

- Is trust the most important thing in a relationship? Many people say that trust is the #1 characteristic they want in a partnership. Many experts believe that trust and trustworthiness are the most important characteristics people want in a partner.

- What breaks trust in a relationship? Trust is broken when one partner puts his or her own needs and desires ahead of what's best for the relationship. Trust is also broken when partners break their promises or violate important expectations.

- Can you love someone and not trust them? Some experts say we can only truly love someone we can trust. What do you think and believe? I believe trust is earned through actions and words, because just saying words can sound like empty promises. For me I want and need the person's words and behaviors to match. Congruency is what helps build trust in my relationships.

- Can the way we think and act compromise the trust we have in our partner? Our own doubt and fears can play a part in hindering our ability to trust, even when our partner shows us they can be trusted.
We have to be aware of the times when we are demanding that our partner pay for the sins of the past, and recognize how this can effect the trust relationship. No one likes being accused of doing what "the other" person "used to do." Not only is this unfair to our partners, but it hinders our ability to trust.

- What to do when you don't trust your partner? Be open, honest, and acknowledge feelings and practice being vulnerable. Communicate about key issues in your relationship. Acknowledge how past hurts may be triggering mistrusts in the current relationship. Listen to your partners side of the story.

- How to build trust in a relationship:

    Say what you mean and mean what you say.

    Gradually allow yourself to be vulnerable.

    Be respectful.

Give the benefit of the doubt.

Express your feelings even when it's tough to do so.

Take a risk together.

Be willing to give as well as receive.

- What are the four aspects of trust?
Consistency

Compassion

Communication

Competency

Every element is an important part of having a trusting relationship with another person.

Chapter 7: Active Listening

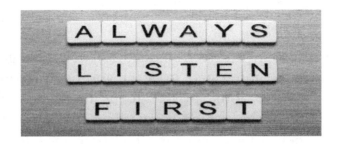

Being a good listener improves relationships you have with people in your life. Genuinely listening to other people helps them to realize you care about them. Being a good listener is not always easy. Often, we are thinking of our responses while the other person is still talking. Here are a few helpful hints to being a good listener.

- Choose to be intentionally present. With approximately 6.4 billion people worldwide using smartphones and other devices, it can take effort to be present with the person right in front of you. If you want to be a better listener, turn off your devices or at the very least silence them.

- Eliminate distractions and focus on the person who is talking. If you are not meeting in person and are talking to someone on the phone, don't be tempted to check your email on your devices or you will lose focus. You can only listen intently when you are not distracted.

- Become an open-minded listener. It is good to be interested in what another person is saying. Some people focus more on being interesting which means they talk more than they listen. Be quick to listen and slow to speak and learn to ask open ended questions. Seek first to understand instead of being understood. Create a safe environment for the other person to feel heard and valued. Being genuinely interested in the other person's perspective and this will cause them to trust you and share openly and honestly.

- Be empathetic and never judge. Listening is an act of empathy as you try and see a situation through another person's eyes. It is important to understand how they are feeling. If you are judging them while they are talking, they are not going to open up to you in an honest manner. Extend respect, kindness, compassion, grace, forgiveness to the degree that you would like it extended to you.

- Show them that you are listening to what they are saying. Your body language shows how attentive you are to the other person. Make eye contact. Lean forward just a bit, and maybe nod some. Again, avoid thinking about what you will say next in your response to them.

- Do not talk while the other person is still talking. Always wait for the other person to finish talking before commenting or asking them a question. It can be rude to stop them mid-sentence acting like what you have to say is more important than what they are in the middle of saying. If you do not understand what they are saying, it is okay to ask them to repeat what they have said. Also, you can tell them what you think you heard them say to ensure that you have fully understood them.

- Become a safe listener. Pay attention to yourself as you listen to your partner. Are you waiting for a pause so you can jump in with your "wise advice" which your partner probably believes in criticism or nagging? Suspended judgment when listening to others is a must if you want them to continue talking with you. Remember when you are a safe listener, it is not about you it is about paying close attention to what they are saying verbally and non-verbally.

Psst. ......It wasn't the

trauma that made you

stronger, kinder, and more empathetic --

it's how you handled it.

That credit is yours.

Chapter 8: Signs of a Loving Relationships

What does a truly loving relationship look like? First, figure out who you are and what you stand for; then and only then will you be ready to venture out into being yourself in a healthy relationship.

In a loving relationship, strive for a healthy, honest, respectful, inclusive, joyful, loving, relationship that values and promotes individual expression and personal growth for both individuals. It is also important to have intimacy, friendship, familiarity, and connections that are different than the ones you have with other family members.

Goals:

- **Participate in each other's growth and development.** Learn from the feelings and behaviors of your partner and gain new or different perspectives. Your partner's interests may serve as an opportunity to help you learn and grow.

- **Value and respect each other's individuality and boundaries.** Understand we are all different, and that does not mean one person is "less than." Instead look for opportunities to gain insight into the other person's perspective. In a healthy, loving relationship you respect your partner's boundaries. Give each other space away from the relationship to be with friends, pursue interests, and to have some alone time.

- **Communicate in a healthy manner.** Feel free and comfortable to say what is on your mind. Do not think you and your partner will agree on everything, because you will not. Keep communication honest and straightforward. No criticizing, no judging, no shaming, and no blaming. Listen to what your partner is really saying both verbally and nonverbally.

- **Share similar values.** Best case scenario you are both on the same page about the important issues. Having a similar way of looking at things like family values, raising children, and religious/spiritual beliefs creates opportunities to relate to one another on important issues.

- **Trust each other without question.** Trust means you believe your partner has what it takes to stay in the relationship. Trust implies the healthy relationship is unshakable and your partner will remain loyal to you. Trust includes honoring your commitments, not lying, and remaining open to working out difficulties that come up.

- **Share major life decisions.** Problems will come up during any relationship, but no one partner should call all the shots. Work together as a team in order to work out solutions that best meet the needs of the relationship. Learning how to give and take is a very important process in problem-solving. Make sure both partners contribute equally to making major decisions and choices.

- **Do your best to let things go and move on.** Change and transition are inevitable, nothing stays the same even if we want it to. There will be disappointments, frustrations for what life throws your way, but a loving healthy relationship teaches us that standing together and moving forward together helps us successfully reach what is waiting for us on the other side. Healthy teamwork provides strength and balance.

Where red and yellow flags can indicate an unhealthy relationship, a loving relationship is filled with green flags. Some green flags are:

- They celebrate your wins.
- They remember small things about you.
- They respect your boundaries.
- They respect you and your goals.
- They listen without being defensive.
- They are not judgy and don't promote shame or guilt.
- You feel safe in their presence.
- You don't have to watch every word you say around them.
- You feel energized after seeing them.
- You enjoy making decisions together.
- They make you want to be a better person.
- You really like you when you are with them.

"Love is a two-way street constantly under construction."

●

"Sometimes, things don't work out. Not because you don't deserve it, but because you deserve so much more."

"Be kind to others wherever and whenever you can."

–Julie W. Hubbs, M.S.

www.AboutProgressNotPerfection.com

Made in the USA
Columbia, SC
21 June 2025